T0113553

Poetry From the Soul

John Merisko

authorHOUSE®

AuthorHouse™
1663 Liberty Drive
Bloomington, IN 47403
www.authorhouse.com
Phone: 833-262-8899

Published by AuthorHouse 09/07/2023

ISBN: 978-1-6655-6228-7 (sc)
ISBN: 978-1-6655-6229-4 (e)

Contents

About the Author

"I...I start at the beginning.
I write for myself, my wife, and my children.
For this is my love to you."

John was a good, kind man who will be remembered as
a devoted husband and father, a
dedicated teacher to his students, and a devout Christian
who loved his God.
Enjoy "Poetry from the Soul"
The Merisko Family

Preface

The poet in his solitude,
Uses his words as tools.
He crafts a rhyming tale of emotion
That touches the soul of the readers.

The poet is a man's conscience.
In turn, he is the conscience of his society.
A culture without a poet is as barren as the desert.

The poet in his profundity,
Attempts to steer the direction of his reader.
His handicap is whether he is heard, or will be heard.
By enough of the masses to make a difference.

I, in my vain attempt,
Pretend to imitate the poet.
Perhaps, a word spoken,
Or written,
May one day serve to alter the course of
One man's behavior.

Then perhaps, the infection will spread,
To change the direction of a society,
And eventually affect the future of mankind.

John Merisko

"You give up little when you give up your possessions.
It is when you give of yourself that you truly give."

-Kahlil Gibran

I share with you some thought I think,
When I am all alone.
I place them upon a page,
And fashion them into poems.
The greatest joy of all my work,
Is sharing them with friends.
I hope that you will read them.
My soul to you I lend.

I Found a Stone

I found a stone upon my walk,
And understand God's work of art.
Cleverly carved by endless wear,
It summoned me to stop and stare.

Unique it was as all things are,
Beckoning like some distant star.
A simple stone I thought at first,
Those hidden secrets masked its birth.

How much in common we each shared,
God's plan divine was now laid bare.
Tempered by time and made of clay,
Each a part of the Genesis day.

Creation's artwork on display,
Her gallery gracing heaven's gate.
I found a stone upon my walk,
And understood God's work of art.

My Heart

There is a place within my heart,
Where only Jill resides.

There is a place within my heart,
Where Jeanne likes to hide.

There is a place within my heart,
Where it is filled with Joy.

The other place that can be found,
Play John, my only boy.

My Book

Lost magic found between the folds,
Can sever bonds and free the soul.
Hour by our the tale entwines,
And whisks me to another time.

Wondrous tales of life unfold,
Weaving plots for young and old.
Dragons, wizards, castles, and kings,
Glancing deer, a bird on the wing.

Journey's beginning as in life,
Feeds the curious appetite.
Another time, another place,
Freeing me from my bounded space.

I read of tales in far off land,
Where dreamers shape the fate of man.
Where noble men do meet and plot,
Upon a land called Camelot.

Crimson binders ingrained with gold,
Reveal a tale, as yet, untold.
Aging parchment stained with ink,
Awakes the mind to stir and think.

Of golden sunsets on the sea,
Where sailors die and loved ones grieve.
Where lovers love and dreamers dream.
Where poets rhyme and schemers scheme.

Where young brides wed and babies make.
Where mother's hand the cradle shakes.
When boys were young and spirits high,
And men saw visions in the sky.

So on I read into the night.
New knowledge whets my appetite.
Page on page, adventures abound,

Lost in Light the Reader is Found

Shadows grow long and dim the sight.
Fireflies and moonbeams light the nights.
Flickering candles guide my eyes.
Starlight seeks out a place to hide.

Weary eyes that invite the sleep,
Cut the light, discovering peace.
Drawn reflects on the winding brook,
And now at rest, I close my book.

My Garden

I have a little garden where flowers never grow.
I do not even plow or weed, and seeds I never sow.
My harvest does not come in fall,
It always comes in spring.
I grow what people cannot see,
I nurture human beings.

I teach them that the light of life,
Is wisdom to be gained.
That knowledge must be mastered,
And nourished by the rain.
The rain of discipline washes off
The idle hands of man.
And stays them on their steady course,
To say, "I also ran."

The soil of discovery, will spur them on their way.
To harvest dreams, as yet undreamed,
And visions in latter days.
And in the autumn of their stay,
Like changing leaves in fall,
The color of their wisdom flowers
Best when heaven calls.

When I was Young

When I was young I used to dream,
Of golden sunbeams in the spring.
Of falling water, crystal clear,
Of sun kissed roses you held dear.
The scent of lilacs fresh with dew,
The sparrow's song that we once knew.
It seems to me like yesterday,
When you and I were young.

And now that we are growing old,
Our skies have turned from blue to gold.
The sands of time have slipped away,
But our true love will never fade.
And when our final sunset comes,
I pray that we will still be one.
To spend eternity with you,
And be forever young.

Tugs Upon the Heartstrings

As I awoke, I found my heart
In pieces on the ground.
The time it broke I know not when,
It didn't make a sound.
Some say that hearts are made of love,
And tears will cleanse the soul,
But time will wear most anything,
And age will take its toll.

It must have happened long ago,
When I was very young.
Those darts of hate that people threw,
Were only meant in fun.
As time went by the love it held,
Began to slip away.
Instead of growing stronger,
My heart began to fade.

Did they not understand that hearts,
Are fastened to the soul,
By strings of love that babies tug,
And children like to hold.
A simples glance of one's own child,

Can tug upon those strings,
Which causes hurt upon the heart,
And starts the pain to sting.

But wise men say that hearts can mend,
If others love us more.
That hearts stay strong and do not break,
When all the love is stored.
Perhaps my heart can heal itself
If I perchance to try,
To love my fellow man and beast,
And children til I die.

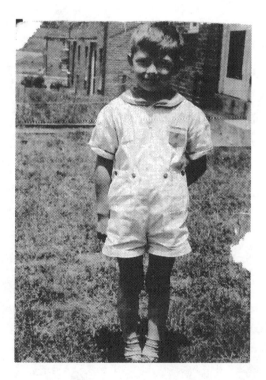

The Passerby

I sat alone upon a stone,
And in my hands I wept.
A passerby sat by my side,
And in my past he crept.

I shared with him my saddest tale,
Of how my daughters three,
No longer dwelt within my house,
But stole their love from me.

They gave their love to three young lads,
I never knew them well.
But by some magic dust of love,
They seemed to cast a spell.

And now I am alone you see,
Within an empty nest.
These walls that echoed laughter,
Have now been put to rest.

The passerby with outstretched hands,
Began to speak his mind.
Did you not give your heart sway,
When you were in your prime?

In time your daughters will comes back,
With lovers by their sides,
Bearing babies that will melt your heart,
And end your foolish pride.

I dried my tears and left the stone.
The passerby had vanished.
But long remembered were his words,
That love you cannot manage.

Nighttime

Each night as sleep invades my realm
And I upon my pillow lay,
My thoughts are numbered one by one,
Then each begins to fade.
Hovering angels overhead,
Descend to rest upon my bed.
And stay their vigil through the night,
That I may sleep til morning's light.

And so to sleep, and in my dreams,
I'm lifted by an angel's wing.
And carried to a place unknown,
To see my God upon his throne.
The King of Kings looks down to see,
A wanton sinner such as me.
God's grace bestowed upon my brow,
I take my leave and gently bow.

His warming glance creates a glow,
Encouraging my stay,
But return I must to mortal life,
To await my judgement day.

His presence fills my soul with joy,
An eternal gift I treasure,
That I may feel the sense of God,
Is one of life's great pleasures.

Slipping down the troth of sleep,
My heart slows to a deathlike beat.
Throughout the night my sleep is stirred,
By whispering angels overheard.
And in the morn when I awake,
The light of dawn will warm my face,
God's grace upon me I will wear,
To greet the new day with a prayer.

God's Perfection

Winter is her naked time,
The winds about her swirl.
She wears the snow about her bough,
Like braided strands of pearls.

But soft, the April winds do blow,
Foretelling the end of winter's snow.
And kissed by gentle winds of spring,
Awakens from her winters dream.

Her thirst for rain and light of day,
Will burst the flowers that bloom in May,
She celebrates her zest for life,
Releasing seeds that soar in flight.

She bows to the wind like some lacy shroud,
And stretches to reach the passing clouds,
And in her crown she dawns her gems,
Of sparrows, skylarks, robins, and wrens.

She tempers the sun with cooling shade,
Where on my knees I come to pray.
She does not lust and sin like me,
She's God's perfection,
She is a tree.

Beach Boy

My love, the poet speaks of the sea.
My love, the poet speaks of thee.
My love, the boy who combs the beach,
For hidden secrets beyond his reach.

He sifts the ageless grains of sand,
For nature's treasures in his hand.
Too young to really understand,
His query for the promised land.

Shimmering light like flakes of gold,
Dims a day that now grows old.
Skipping across a dancing sea,
Stirring a young boy's fantasy.
Melodious tones of a sea that glistens,
Heard by a boy who chose to listen.
To the rush of the wind, and the waves that tumble,
To the cry of the piper, and the crash of thunder.

The subtle waves lap at his feet,
As if to say, come let us meet.
Do not tarry, for life is short.
Your friend I'll be til you reach port.

From sea to shore the boy will roam,
Til heaven calls and beckons him home.
Loving the sea and loving thee,
His life will be brief, his soul will be free.

The Rose

Most beautiful flower the rose in bloom,
Displays her might in early June.
Painting the landscape with rainbow hues,
Wet to the touch of morning's dew.

A harbinger of spring sent as a gift,
To remind us that love will ever exist.
Beckoning lovers to come and see,
The colors of her tapestry.

The rose whose petals these lips have kissed,
Will fade like the fog of a morning's mist.
And lest ye fail her beauty remembered,
She will return in sweet September.

A token of love for all who marry,
A lift of regret for those who tarry.
A lift of joy garnished with sorrow,
Rekindling love in every tomorrow.

Speak to me, o rose in bloom,
For nature's beauty do I swoon.
Oh rose, oh rose, oh rose in bloom,
Have I but loved too little, too soon?

The opiate of her fragrance
Intoxicates my will,
And softly whispers to my heart,
Be still, be still, be still.

A symbol of love for all who dare,
To surrender the heart to those who care.
Upon her flower I will but gaze,
To lavish love with endless praise.

O naked rose when full in bloom,
Thou doth blind the eye to sin.
Do prime the heart of my fair maid,
And will my love, her heart to win.

So run to find the love of your life,
And with a rose, make her your wife.
That for your love, she will but swoon,
When a rose you present in June.

And when in hand a rose you hold,
Tell her you love her, for no mortal knows,
When her petals will fade and die,
Her fragrance remembered with a sigh.

The Rainbow

Softly through God's prism flows
A ray of light that scatters so,
And rests upon the landscape high
A rainbow born upon the sky.

From heaven sent through the mist and rain
God's promise of eternal gain,
For all who design may come and see
The hand of creativity.

Beyond the storminess of night
The rainbow will appear in light.
Guiding all through life's cruel maze
A beacon for the soul to save.

The treasures found at rainbow's end
Are powers that heal the soul to mend.
No gold or silver will you sow
But acts of love that best eh soul.

Resting on white pillowed clouds
The rainbow sleeps but for a while.
As in life the beauty fades
Into the twilight of her age.

Rainbow come and rainbow glow,
To vanish like the melting snow.
The colors strewn upon the sky
Will dress the wings of butterflies.

The rainbow lives where bluebirds fly
And puffs of white adorn the sky.
It lives where all our dreams come true,
Where angels sleep on fields of blue.

The Wooden Rocking Chair

There is a wooden rocking chair
That was bequeathed to me.
It sits within a corner
And haunts my memory.

Now when the rocker do I glance.
My thoughts slip to a richer time.
When laughter sailed upon the wind,
And innocence was prime.

It happened many years ago
In a place not far away.
A land called Terabithia,
Where only children play.

Well remembered were the days
When children found were lost in play.
Not counting seconds,
Nor even minutes,
Or how many hours in the day.

The memory of a brother lost
Is a grief one should not bear.
But soothing is his gift of love,
The wooden rocking chair.

The Joy B

There is a little fishing boat
That floats upon the sea.
Whose ergo holds a treasure chest
Of cherished memories.

Recall the times of bygone days
When on the sea we came to play.
A time remembered when father and son
Would sail the bea to bond as one.

Down to the sea my son and me,
Down to the sea where winds blow free.
To bond as father and son should be,
The wind, the sea, my son and me.

The treasured catch was not the fish,
But the miracle of a father's wish.
To strengthen the heartstrings of father and son
With knots of love that will not be undone.

Down to the sea, my son and me,
Down to the sea where dreams roam free.
Floating upon a tranquil seas,
The wind, the sea, my son and me.

My son no longer fishes the sea.
Loneliness is my destiny
Until the day when we are free
To fish on God's eternal sea.

I See God

From heaven sent by God to me,

A soul that lives eternally,

With inner eye no man perceives, a gift that for myGod I see.

He glows within the blush of dawn. His breath the

summer breeze so calm.

I see God in the nighttime sky, when dimmest star

my eye doth spy.

I see God in the burst of spring when hummingbirds

return to sing,

When flowers bright their colors bleed, painting nature's

tapestry.

I see God in the summer flow. He rides upon the driven

snow

And tumbles with the fallen rain to cleanse the soul

of sin and pain.

I see God in the twilight flow, where nights are born

and days grow old.

When stars awaken from their sleep and angel's through

their windows peek.

I see God in the afterglow, creating shadows far below.

A place where only lovers hide, their secret masked

from probing eyes.
He hides within the fresh baked bread, a loving mother's
hand did tread,
With face of love and kindly care, her humble life
a living prayer.

When through a dewdrop do I peer, host of angels hover
near,
Against a golden sky they rise, disguised as colored
butterflies.
When through a teardrop do I peer, host of angels
gather near,
Praising God on bended knee, but for my inner eye
I see.
Oh Rouge of Heaven blood red thou art, would thoubut heal this
wounded heart.
The wine that drips upon my tongue, pray keep my soul
forever young.

Oh death will thou not seek me out. God's mercy will
expel my doubt.
Wilt thou be kind to this old man, who hungers for
the Promised Land.
I see God in the eyes of love, sent through tears
from those above.
Like graceful flights of mourning doves,
I see my God in those I love.

Babaland

As autumn leaves without a sound
Fall ever gently to the ground,
They seek a bed on which to rest
Upon the earth's caressing breast.

So as a child I too did roam,
To find a place to call my own.
A place where wanting arms of love
Embrace me with a thousand hugs.

Hitching a dream to the rising sun,
I fly until the day is done.
Gliding along on gossamer wings
I soar to where the angels sing.

And come to rest upon a hill,
Garnished with fields of daffodils.
And there a lady so warm and then,
Soon would become my very best friend.

Wrinkled hand that shaped my fate
Still hold my love to keep it safe.
I bask within a sea of love,
Embraced by arms of a Baba's hug.

As thistle seeds do seek to roam
To find a place to call their own,
So as a child I too did roam
And found a place to call my home.

And what the hands so soft embraced,
Did plow life's furrows with her grace.
Crafted by a Baba's hand,
An island of love called Babaland.

God's Speed

The trenches stained, run red with blood.
The shallow graves are full.
The nature of untimely deaths,
Is tragic and most cruel.

No anger dwells within the hearts,
Of those who came to die.
The laughter of those brave young lads,
Still echoes through the sky.

Of mothers, how they grieve for sons,
No dreams fulfilled, no race to run.
Like pawns upon the game of life,
They made the holy sacrifice.

A hero's death to be remembered,
If only in a song,
That living comrades come to sing,
For heroes that are gone.

So gather round these herald lambs,
And pray them to the Promised Land.
One by one their sins are purged,
By the cadence of the funeral dirge.

One, one...one, two, three,
One, one...one, two, three,
One, one...one, two, three,
One, one...one, two, three.

Bluebird of Happiness

There is a little bluebird
Who sits upon my sill,
And sings such songs of happiness,
With love my heart doth fill.

A symphony of joy he brings
To ears that once were closed,
With songs of spring that lovers sing,
Of quiet sweet repose.

He sings of spring when fields turn green,
And life begins to stir,
Awakening the heart to sing,
Of maiden's love so fair.

He sits upon my shoulder,
And whispers in my ear,
That all the joy within one's heart,
Is found when love is near.

He came from where I do not know,
But this I tell you true,
That since he chose to grace my life,
My skies have all been blue.

And then one day he went away,
And never said goodbye.
And now I sit beside my sill,
And cry, and cry, and cry.

Oh bird of paradise sing me home,
That I may hear your lovely tones.
Pleasing to my ear they are,
I will but love thee from afar.

The Butterfly

Summer snowflakes dress the sky,
And dart in staggered flight.
Born from fading rainbows end,
To appear as butterflies.

Winged colors best the summer's glow,
And strain to swagger to and fro.
Wings that fan the hopes of men,
Searching for a wanting friend.

And when the butterfly we meet,
Presents us with a kiss,
It may be just as act of love,
From those we sorely miss.

As snowflakes fall and crowd to melt,
The butterfly will bring,
The breath of God, of love, or life,
His praise for all to sing.

Oh butterfly, oh butterfly,
Come share your kiss with me,
That all may now this act of love,
Will last eternally.

The Fisherman

The fisherman awake at dawn,
And scurries to his favorite pond.
There he sits alone at last,
Trolling for the elusive bass.

And all the while he contemplates,
The path that brought him to this place.
A road still strewn with hopes and dreams,
Wonders of what the future brings.

Mistakes of youth still haunt his dreams.
Innocence fades in the scheme of things.
A litany of sins have traversed his path,
A restful conscience is in his past.

Regrets renewed, his time is spent,
Let memories fade, lest ye lament.
Garnished by sorrow and a rain of tears,
A faith in God to soften his fears.

He did not write the book of time.
Only God could be so kind.

The Author of Life will pen his name,
One heaven's golden window pane.

As in life, disappointments abound.
Today the fish are not to be found.
He will return at the break of dawn,
To revisit his soul at his favorite pond.

Broken Hearted

Judge me not too harshly, Oh ye of noble fare,
The blood that courses through your veins is purest
and most rare.
Your mighty homes are made of stone, with towers thatspike the sky.
Such riches are unknown to me. A poor man will Idie.

Can I but dream of treasures, to place before your
eyes,
To tempt the palate of your heart, and steal you to
my side.
If love had wings or spirits sing, songs would fly
into your heart.
The love that we will never share, keeps us so far
apart.

Perhaps the love that could have been, was never meant
to be.
But by some magic quirk of fate, belies our destiny.
The distance of our love is strained, for we shall
never meet,
To savor all the joys of life, into eternity.

Upon a bed of straw I'll lie, beneath a starry sky.
To dream of love that could have been, will haunt
me til I die.
Adrift upon the sea of life, a ship without a rudder,
Will find my broken heart alone,
To never love another.

Fallen Angel

I know not of the ways of love,
Or how we came to be.
I know I did not fall in love,
But love fell into me.

From high above an angel fell,
And nestled to my side,
And whispered softly in my ear,
That she would be my bride.

Into my heart with gentle hand,
My love she did embrace,
And like some cunning rogue with wings,
Alas my love did take.

As gentle summer rains do quench,
The thirst of promised life,
The shower of love will ever bathe,
Our hearts in lasting light.

The Cinder and the Tear

The cinder is a speak of clay,
A part of God's creation.
The tear can cleanse the sins of man,
And grant him his salvation.
The cinder irritates the eye,
The tear can only heal.
But cinders do not feel the pain,
That only time reveals.

The origin of the cinder has,
From fiery rock been formed.
The tear from glaciers origin,
But by the heart is born.
If cinders are the sins of man,
That lead to one's damnation,
Then tears must be the saving grace,
That quiets all temptation.

Cinder are distinctive,
Inflicting only pain.
But tears have many origins,
That one cannot explain.

The tears of joy are often seen,
As when a babe is born.
But suffer not the sorrow tears,
As when the heart is torn.

As in the past when first I lived,
And wanting was my pleasure,
I chose the path that hastened me,
To search for life's small treasures.
On judgement day when all is done,
The tears of joy will flow,
And douse the fiery cinder,
That burn in hell below.

My Secret Hiding Place

Where is this place that's oh so safe?
Where all my treasures hide?
Where gold and pearls and rubies placed,
Have vanished from my eyes.

I put them a novel place,
Remembered for a day.
But when they are to be retrieved,
My memory starts to fade.

I've search and searched but cannot find,
Those misplaced valued jewels.
My secret through, if truth be told,
Is mortals are such fools.

Transgressing all of time and space,
I know one things is clear,
That all of my life's treasures,
Have somehow disappeared.

Perhaps one day, by happenstance,
If I am yet to be,
I'll find my misplaced treasures,
And set my mind at ease.

On Love

If all the world were at my feet,
And all life's treasures gained,
What small reward would this all be?
If love were not to blame.

If flowers could blossom in the snow,
Or out of ashes grow,
Would not my life be better served?
If winds of love could blow.

If time stood still, the day of sun,
Forever would shine bright.
How sad for lovers that the moon.
Would never flow at night.

If one's reflection in a pool,
Smiles back at every age,
What secrets must our mirrors hold,
What falsehoods grace our face?

If dreams and wishes all came true,
And joys of life are given,
When all our wants in life are filled,
Is there a need for living?

If drops of water spawn a lake,
Or grains of sand a beach,
Could not be kindness by a foe,
Grow into lasting peace?

And in the twilight of our stay,
When recollections fade,
Will one remember all the good,
That memories can save?

The final bell that tolls for me,
Will be a brisk new sound,
Vibrating through the crisp fall air,

While I am heaven bound.

Love of a Father

I felt the pain within my chest,
I could not think to pray.
I knew that I would see my God,
On this my judgement day.
And angel took me by the hand,
My wife and children cried.
I told them all I loved them
Just before I died.

But in the morning when I wake,
My angel was my nurse.
Saint Peter was my doctor
His prayers were answered first.
My family smiled through all their tears
And reinforced their love,
With never ending kisses,
And thirty thousand hugs.

The Poet's Lament

Whose words these are the poet plots,
His pen, the brush that prints the thoughts.
His canvas is the scroll unmarked.
Painted images be doth wrought.

The barren desert wants for rain.
The price of rhyming, constant pain.
Words come slow and ideas weak,
The mind is parched and will not speak.

Emotions are deafening without a voice.
The poet's hand must make a choice.
At last the words race to the page.
Rhythm measured acts as a gauge.

The author must hurry before the drought.
Ideas are flying and must be caught.
Selected worlds must first be tamed,
And laid in place to complete the frame.

Candles burn low, colors are bright
Painted words light up one's life.
Yellow for light and red for pain,
White for the bride and blue for the rain.

Search no more, the task is complete.
The poet can rest, his page is replete.
Tomorrow's dawn will find him alone,
Sifting the words for another poem.

The Pumpkin Patch

There is a little patch of ground,
Where only pumpkins grow.
How many can be counted,
No one will ever know.
They sleep upon a bed of green,
Caressed by sun and rain,
To one day be a jack-o-lantern,
In my window pane.

Precious Baby

Precious baby dressed in pink,
Can you tell me what you think?
Are the stars in heaven bright?
Did God make you out of light?

Precious baby, dressed in blue,
Can you love as I love you?
Will the heaven's trumpets sound,
When on earth at last you're found?

Precious baby, dressed in white,
Do the angels sing in flight?
Will your skies be always blue,
Will your love for life be true?

Precious baby, dressed in gold,
Do not cry when you I hold.
Will the angel's sound their horns,
When like Jesus you are born?

Precious baby, dressed in lace,
Did God bless you with His grace?
May your cross be always bright,
Returning you to heaven's light.

The Moth

Attracted by the light of fire,
The moth fulfills his last desire.
Toward the danger flown in frenzied state,
The final act will seal his fate.

The Serpent

The serpent crawls upon the ground.
He moves without a single sound.
Into a hole he curls and hides,
Protected from my watchful eye.

The Swinger

I got rhythm.
I buy shoes,
I go dancing to the blues.

I make a fool.
Girls don't drool,
Call me goofy,
That is cruel.

I sell shoes.
I stay home.
Me and dog are all alone.

Goodbye

The boy who played within my heart,
No longer can be found.
The time he left I know not when,
He did not make a sound.

He did not stop to say goodbye,
No hug or kiss had he.
He simply left his love for mom,
And blessed his sisters three.

The Crown Prince

Go forth sweet prince and tarry not, the angels singthee home.
Summoned by the God most high, to see what thou hast
sown.
At journey's end the prize is won, so lift your trophyhight,
That all may see the newest star shining in the sky.

Seek not to know the reason why God called for oneso young.
Find solace in his finest hour, the distance of his
run,
He may be gone but not for me,
I see him all the while.
He hides within his mother's tear and in his sisters'
smiles.

Suffer not the pangs of guilt no grieve too much forme,
The splendor of the love you gave will last eternally.
You always ran the high road and walked the extramile,
Searching for the ways of man and clinging to their
style.

Tethered to our hearts by love with strings that singwith pain,
He searched the foreign lands with ease and walkeddown life's own
lanes.
Recall him as the Prince of Life, his quest had justbegun.
Find solace in his golden year,his goals, the race
he won.

At rainbow's end where poppies grow and violets bed
the lamb,
We'll meet again and talk as friends in this, ourhappy land.
Fault im not for he was mortal his destiny fulfilled,
The King of Terabithia, finally revealed.

I Don't Know

Do I sing because I'm happy,
Or am I happy because I sing?

Am I tired because I'm sleepy,
Or am I sleepy because I'm tired?

Do i love because I am loved,
Or am I loved because I love?

Do i cry because I'm sad,
Or am I sad because I cry?

Do I dance because I am happy,
Or am I happy because I dance?

Do I age because I am old,
Or am I old because I age?

Do I wait because I am patient,
Or am I patient because I wait?

Am I tall because I'm a wall,
Or amI a wall because I am tall?

Do I laugh because it's funny,
Or is it funny because I laugh?

Do I pray because I am holy,
Or am I holy because I pray?

I Don't Know Either

Do I sin because I'm bad,
Or am I bad because I sin?

Do I forgive because I am forgiven,
Or am I forgiven because I forgive?

Do I wear a crown because I am a King,
Or am I a King because I wear a crown?

Am I poor because I have no wealth,
Or do I have no wealth because I am poor?

Am I a poet because I rhyme,
Or do I rhyme because I am a poet?

Do I love because I am good,
Or am I good because I love?

Do I nurture because I am a parents,
Or am I a parent because I nurture?

Do I sin because I am shackled,
Or am I shackled because I sin?

Am I generous because I give,
Or do I give because I am generous?

The Easter Bunny

The Easter bunny wear a bow,
Around her furry neck.
She brings us candy jelly beans,
And colored eggs with specks.
Our baskets full are made of straw,
All trimmed in pink and green,
She only comes when flowers grow,
And birds come home to sing.

She hops along a flowered path,
Where periwinkles grow.
And feeds upon the rabbitbrush,
When warmer winds do blow.
She shares with us her thoughts of love,
And pastels to be viewed.
Shell bring to us the sweetest gift,
The promise of life renewed.

The Race

I ran the race and ran it hard,
I did not stop to rest.
The pounding of my blistered feet,
Was felt within my chest.
Falling more than once or twice,
My knees were filled with blood.
To ease the pain that wrecked my nerve,
I doused them in some mud.

And deep within my chest I felt,
The thumping of my pride.
If I should never win a race,
I'll know that I have tried.
The desert run, with burning feet,
The mountains high I've climbed,
And touched the clouds that God has made,
To reach the finish line.

The Cleansing

Suffer not the pain of sin, that I may taste the grace
of God.
Hunger not for worldly wants, divorce me from that
fraud.
Cleanse my tongue of cursed phrases, that words may
flow as prayers.
Strip me of my lust and hate, that for my brother
I may care.

Purge my jealous heart that beats, a thousand sins
a day,
And fill it with the love of God, that I may never
stray.
Wash away suspicion, that trust will never stray.
Then anger will begin to die, moaning like the beast.

Strip me of my nakedness, for all who want may see,
That only through His wisdom, befalls my destiny.
I was a gift when I was borne, a gift of life to all,
But not to be surrendered, to sin I will not fall.

May the waters of theJordan help to purify my sin.

God's grace is everlasting, and draws me close toHim.

May His finger point the way for me, and raise meto the clouds.

Enjoying victory over sin, to touch the hem of God.

Carpe Diem

Winters are cold,
Dragging far into spring.
Save for the warmth of the hearth,
And the affections of my love,
I would not survive.

I collect some logs and offer them to the hearth.
It rewards me with the comfort of heat to warm mybody.
Embracing my wife, I gently kiss her brow.
She rewards me with a tender love which warms my soul.

The smell of brewed coffee floods the kitchen,
Awakening the brain to stir,
Soon to warm the belly.
It strips away the layers of sleep,
Which grow through the night.
The remnants of sleep,
Melt into puddles on the floor.

My heart is warm,
I am now awake,
I am ready to
Seize the day.

My Prayer

Oh Jesus of Nazareth,
You who made th lame to walk,
The blind to see, the dumb to speak,
And rose Lazarus from the dead,
Have mercy on us.
May the sacrificial blood of Calvary,
Rain upon us,
To heal our bodies,
Purify our hearts,
And sanctify our souls.

Amen.

My Neighbor

There is a little lady,
Who lives next door to me,
Why heaven sent her down to us,
Is still a mystery.

She does not walk on water,
But dances on our hearts,
To give our shallow mundane lives,
A stimulating spark.

She forms a type of fairy ring,
Surrounding those she loves,
And captures all the happy times,
To sedn to God above.

The wood nymph flits from log to log,
She skips from friend to friend,
Spreading to all the grace of God,
Praying their souls to mend.

She does not wear a halo,
At least that one can see.
The circle of love about her head,
Is obvious to me.

Reflections

Reflections in your tears revealed,
The ache that swells the heart.
No poem, no song or prose consoles,
The pain that grief hath wrought.

Unless perfaps it was the warm,
Embrace of friends so true,
Who wrapped their arms around me,
And whispered, "I love you."

The weight upon my soul was eased,
When in your eyes I gazed,
And saw the tender love you felt,
For John in bygone days.

You welcomed John into your home,
And loved him like a son.
Your concern for him, the love you shared,
Will cheer the race he won.

Friends

The gentle winds forever blow,
In all directions to and fro.
They sail from far across the sea,
To settle gently as a breeze.

Like the wind you too did roam,
Until at last you found a home.
Up the hill and around the benc,
You finally met a lasting friend.

Like the wind you began to soar,
To find yourself at John's front door.
His welcome war warm, you were his delight,
He captured an angel and halted its flight.

You found our son John, noble indeed,
A friend to fulfill your destiny.
His carm was seductive, his demeanor would please,
His only fault was he liked to tease.

Hugs and kisses were not his style,
His greatest strength was his smile.
The pixie grin that he would share,
Could melt the hearts of those who cared.

John spoke of you often in the most glowing of terms.
The fondness you nurtured is a lesson well learned.
I know that he treasured your generous ways,
Remember the good times, you'll see him someday.

The sands of time have slipped away.
But one can only kneel and pray,
Giving thanks for the memories that we so treasure,
Of a man we once knew who gave so much pleasure.

John would become a loving friend.
You continued to charm him until the end.
A truer friend he could not have earned,
His mother and I thank you for your concern.

Jesus Christ is Born

Oh, Silent Night, the Holy Night,
Heaven's Angels are in flight,
Telling all that Jesus Christ is born.

Hosanna to the King of Kings,
Hear the steeple church bells ring,
Telling all that Jesus Christ is born.

Three Wise Men traveled from afar,
To see where Jesus lay.
Guided by the Christmas Star,
They found the new born Babe.

They paid their homage to the King,
And heard the Herald Angels sing,
That our redeemer Jesus Christ was born.

The Crown Prince laid within a crib,
Made from straw and cedar twigs,
Glowing like the stars high up adobe.

The shepherds gathered round to see,
One of God's great mysteries,
God divine had come to earth that day.

Shepherds tending to their flock,
Saw angels in the sky.
They did not know the Prince of Peace,
Had come to earth to die.

To open heaven's gate for me,
Fulfilling all the prophecies,
That Jesus Christ, the son of God is born.

My Captain's Ship

Guided by the pilot's hand,
My captain's ship slips out to sea.
White foamlaps at her bow,
Hisses and returns to the deep.
Majestically she cuts the water in regal silence.
Not really understanding
That I will no longer board her decks.

For me, a love lost,
For her, a lost love.
Does she not have a heart?
She displays no emotion.
I have caressed her to the many years.
My life's ship slips out to sea
And I must remain a spectator.
Along I stand on the shore.
My eyes are filled, my heart is torn.
She has tapped my strength and my will.
For I have grown old and tired.

My spirit rises; her mighty mast
Reaches toward teh sky.
To be young again; to discover
A new future.
What destinations would she provide
For me to undertake.
My life's ship slips out to sea.
I shall miss her.
She has benn my mother's milk,
My mistress.
She has ravaged my body and my soul.
My back grows weak with age
And my will begins to bend.

The time has come to give up
The spirit of wonder and begin anew.
The groan of her list I shall miss.
I watch as she grows smaller

And crosses the horizon,
Sinking into the sea.
My heart sinks into the abyss of nostalgia.
At last her mast dips
And no longer touches the sky.

My captain's ship slips out to sea .
No longer will I grace her deck,
Or crew her mighty heave.
No longer will I steady against
Her creaky list.

She has abandoned me on the shore,
But my heart rides her deck.
Her sails are full and spirits high.
She rushes on with the morning tide.
I will remember my life's work.

My captain's slip slips out to sea.
I shall miss her and
I languish in her memory.
No longer will I engage
In the intercourse of daily strift.
No longer will I harvest the fruit of my labor.
This lady of the sea,
My life's work, has seduced me.

This great love of mine
Has stolen my youth.

The pirate of the sea
Has spurned me like so much refuge on the shore.

The Legend of Garfield Jones

I rise to relate in the most modest of tones,
The notorious legend of Garfeild Jones.
Twas my first day of college and the word was about,
That a vociferous person had started a rout.
The fight was with Evans, the Dean of men.
Garfield would never become his friend.
The trouble you see, was the Garfield was shrewd,
He always ended up winning the feud.
In his frustration the Dean would set traps,
To catch our friend Garfield ensnared like some rat.
But Garfield, that tumultuous Tasmanian Devil,
Would not be caught by the cunning fellow.
Like the northern wind that blows from New Ken,
Garfield, would strike and just vanish again.
If Ray Evans was ever the Dean of Men,
Then Garfield was the Demon of Men.
The trouble he caused was all very honest.
He was just having fun, from September to August.
Like the times he threw food in the dining hall.
He meant no harm, he was having a ball.
Anything for a laugh must have been his theme,
Ray Evans, I think could have ripped out his spleen.

But Garfield went on, by heaven's grace,
To escape Dean Evans and graduate.
He came to West Mifflin, that wind from New Ken,
He came to West Mifflin and started again,
He would do the wrong things in all the right places,
And managed to fire up a few more red faces.
His legend was growing as you all well know.
Those seeds of unrest he continued to sow.
His only salvation was that of his wife,
Whose frustrations began to threaten his life.
Two babies would follow and help tame his style,
And Monica would monitor his every mile.
A married man now he began to mellow and confided.
In me his biology fellow.
It made me feel good to swap wife stories with him.
For twenty-nine wishes,
The first would be to wash his own dishes.
But Jack, he would say, "It's a working agreement."
I would work and he would agree is what he meant.
It's not that he's sloppy or lazy and such,
It's just that he's never had quite the right touch.
I've always enjoyed making his agar plates,
And unlocking his cupboards and loaning him tape.
A cross word or argument we never have had.
And for twenty-nine year, that record ain't bad.
I call him my friend because that's what he is.
I'll miss him the legend, he continues to live.

Heaven's Call

Lay me down gently when I die.
That all may gather to my side.
Upon whose brow the tears will rain,
Easing the heart of grieving pain.
Come gaze upon this lifeless farm,
Sadness bleeds from hearts that mourn.
Memories of friendship fade,
When the body invites the shade.
The strangest thing...i have no fear.
But to, there flows a tiny tear,
That swells along my sullen cheek,
For dreams of life that death did cheat.
Uon a stone it will be carved,
By masons travelling from afar,
An epitaph that speaks of life,
How brief the dance of passing light.
And when beneath the sod I lay,
The ground will cut the light of day.
No sound to teach the muted eare,
No image found within my mirror.
And just outside the carriage awaits,
To summon me to heaven's gate.

Lifted by an angel's wing,
Soon to meet the King of Kings.
And all the while I race to see,
The limits of eternity.
And when angelic trumpets sound,
My love I'll share with Heaven's Hound.

Reaching the Gates

Go rest in peace
Go find your son standing at the gates of heaven
Go find your relief
He's waiting for you with soft resurrection

He can't wait to see you
So you'll run, like you're mad, to heaven's door
And you won't want to be blue
And you won't sin no more

Feeling the rapture frow
A feeling I wish of mine
And now you know
That it's okay to shine

Promise you'll wait for me there?
You'll see the God, and his perfection
Ask him if one day I'll be there
You'll talk with great connection

Your thoughts and fears will disappear
Again, your body will become whole
You'll look at your life, it now becomes clear
It's all inspired by poetry from the soul

Written by :
Pap's youngest granddaughter

Printed in the United States
by Baker & Taylor Publisher Services